Let My Life Speak

Helene Bentley

BookLeaf Publishing

Presentation by *BookLeaf Publishing*

Web: www.bookleafpub.com

E-mail: info@bookleafpub.com

ISBN: 9789357616966

First edition 2022

To my boys, Lloyd, Wade and Jett... my reason for living, laughing, crying and staying real.

ACKNOWLEDGEMENT

To Lloyd, Wade and Jett. You are always on at me to write. Love you to the moon and back.

An Ordinary African Day in May

And on an ordinary African morning in the middle of May
The hand of God presented in tiny human form
With surgeons twice and nurse galore a mixture of medicine and prayer
The clean sharp smell of chemicals and chloroform
Months of fear and anxiety intertwined and tightly held
The experience rendering both the illusion of blessing and curse
Some days one and sometimes both as muscle and tendon swelled
And an answered prayer of life complicit with complications appearing perverse
The body rejecting the life it conceived in a twisted cynical pleasure
As science intervened frantically to preserve that which nature had ordained
A signal and magnitude of my faith been at no time a discernible measure
My despair and sombre anguish captive and by my immeasurable fear restrained

And in that moment, a gurgling cry ushered in the anticipated yet uncertain day
For science and faith, a connected miracle in history, forever the 18th of May.

Loving Me

Oh Lord I look in the mirror and I don't like
what I see
Oh why couldn't I see a more beautiful me?
I don't like my face, my hair and in particular
my nose
You tell me I am a precious flower, hell…I don't
see an English rose!
My daughter you insult me when you question
my immaculate design
Before you came along, I managed just fine
I made the rivers, the mountains, fire, wind and
snow
I am the ultimate architect, remember this when
you feel low
I shaped and made you specifically the way that
you are
And no cloning or science has proven me wrong
thus far
If you were slender and fine with a pouting
model's face
Would you be helping others and still be in the
race
To see heaven on earth and the gospel
proclaimed

And doubting and troubled souls fervently reclaimed
My daughter, I think we both know the answer to that
So, let's cut to the chase and leave the idle chitchat
You are made the way that I want you to be
So, look in the mirror, look hard… what do you see?
Do you see joy in your smile and love in your eyes
This my dear daughter, is for what you must strive
These qualities cannot be changed by surgeon, scepter or knife
They are God given qualities that you must learn in life
So, forget the mirror, don't question my design
You are gentle, kind, gracious and above all… you are mine!

I Whispered your name!

I whispered your name in your mother's ear the day you were first conceived
The blueprint of your DNA was waiting before your life was perceived,
Your parents might not have planned you and you still feel the gap
But don't live in rejection, it's the cunning enemy's trap.

Your mother might not have been perfect, serene the epitome of calm
And it may be that at her hand, you experienced deep emotional harm,
But that pathway although not intentional, has provided a training ground so deep,
That will be your training manual to help others with their mountain, no matter how steep.

So, step outside the boundaries of insecurity, fear and loss
Stand up to the enemy, screw him… you are friends with the boss,
This is the appointed time to stand up, take the mantle and fulfil your cause

For far too long your life has felt worthless,
empty and on perpetual pause.

If you do not rise up and take your rightful place
at the helm
you will live a defeated life, meandering the
enemy's realm,
I have given you the blueprint, I have appointed
you this day,
So, get off the pity train and for God's sake seize
the day.

Go out with prayerful purpose, holy- spirit intent
Let me be your guide, your support, my word
your cement,
As you begin to help those who have suffered
the same
That will be your healing, the leveler of your
great pain.

A Whisper of Hope

I listen to the hum of the birds outside and the
song is a little clearer, almost sweet
The red of the creeper, crimson is a little deeper
than usual, redemption, growth and hope,
The humidity in the air glistens and the hue
dances in clusters of gold, a hypnotic beat
I look outwards, nature mirrors my soul, colors
changing, mingling an inspirational
kaleidoscope.

This year bursts forth with purpose, direction
and tangible intent
Divulging pathways and wooded paths with
moss and earthy moisture,
The trees lining the pathway intertwined and
gnarled, a signature of a youth misspent
Experience and character, compassion and
layers, not formulated from a life in cloister.

I will not regret the decisions and choices or
lament the passing of time and seemingly half
moon
I will stand firm as the lion roars and from its
silence awakes and stands on high,

I will not apologize for the instrument that plays
with a sometimes-eerie tune
My spirit will dance with energy and life, it will
forgive and stand firm, and never will it settle
and comply.

May the fragrance be sweeter, the colors yet
deeper and the choices more
May the people that water the pathway be more
complex and convoluted?
May the challenges that seep through be vast
and the richness of emotions raw
May I live with passionate purpose and precision
intent, a life no longer diluted?

Find your Voice

As the darkness shatters the light
And light gives over to fear and fright,
The spirit whispers in the eye of the storm
This is not my way, this is not the norm.

Don't give in to public belief and view
The tongue of the serpent will derail and skew,
I am the alpha and the omega the beginning and
the end
I am not a whim, a mystical fantasy, a fashion
trend.

Feel my breathe, my whisper in the dark
Let me ignite your passion, power and spark,
Let me guide and inspire, feel my power my
might
Choose life, wisdom, peace, and do what is
right.

Do not dance to the beat of the norm
Oh goodness sake, do not conform,
Life is full of wonder and muse
This is not a dress rehearsal to peruse.

Find your passion, find your voice

You have after all, a choice,
Let the purity and peace whisper in your ear
So that generations forth shall not shed a tear.

Confidence Stolen

I feel dread rise up as my meeting draws near
My palms wet and a deep fog holds my thoughts tight,
Why do I feel so incompetent in the presence of this colleague, my peer?
This uneasy feeling in not natural, surely it is not right.

My colleague greets me in a professional yet unwelcoming tone
The voice is not full of passion, pleasure or disdain,
The words are careful and controlled and I feel so alone
The conversation is hollow, empty words and I feel my enthusiasm drain.

I give ideas that have merit, tried and tested and yet there is this silence from miles away
It seems if every thought I offer up is rejected and has no sounding board,
I ask for information, direction and to be included and my begging becomes a silent prayer

My opinions, thoughts and responses not
welcome, and I feel ignored.

The behavior is not overtly rude, it is subtle, and
the dislike reflected in quiet tone
But the silence speaks deeply, and the stillness
holds my dread and fear,
Stilted conversation, language abrupt awkwardly
echoes through the phone
This person quietly stifling, suffocating all that I
hold dear.

As weeks turns to months and time passes
slowly year in and out
My confidence ebbs and dwindles and
motivation is paused,
I try to initiate warmth to be objective, but any
response is birthed in doubt
And I long for a single word of affirmation not
any significant applause.

And so finally I feel broken, and the fog is thick
and deep
And I am forced to resign, to heal that part of me
which has died,
My self -worth eroded gradually and the pain
emerges as I weep

The experience leaving me empty and
vulnerable, numb inside.

The response I get from this person is none
And so, in parting the feeling of uselessness is
compounded,
No thanks for coming, good luck in the future or
that was fun
And the silence is deafening, my instinct
confirmed and founded.

Oh, to be a Wildflower!

Oh were shall I find thee in the sinking sun?
In crevice and ravine, down low and on high,
Where only sacred species can frolic and run
Where river bed is raging and when it's running dry.

Your delicate little petals that form such precious flowers
In deep purple, lavender, white and every possible hue,
Your lofty head stands gallantly as though you have super powers
Your perfect leaves a vessel to contain both sap and dew.

Your fragrance sweet and delicate wafts across the plain
Your beauty pure and deep, a perpetual delight,
So bountiful in nature and of every perceivable strain
A symphony of pleasure, an extraordinary sight.

If only you could whisper your thoughts and teach me half your know

Of rhythmic seasons rising and falling, of
resilience, hope and emphatic trust,
Knowledge of your perfection, wisdom and
serenity would help my spirit grow
Oh, this reliance on creation, this strength, this
unapologetic presence- this is what I lust.

Where has my boy gone?

I sit in sadness and ponder, on where did my wee lad go
On attaining the teenage year I felt his presence change,
The difference wasn't rapid and swift yet noticeable and slow
His testosterone and pheromones ascending to a tangible range.

His spirit seemed to darken like a cumulonimbus cloud
His sombre mood and negative vibe threatening like a storm,
His shoulders broad and taught to match his eyes steely and proud
Oh where had my sweet boy gone, I did not recognise his new form.

He grew more aloof and menacing and his words were harsh and cold
He seemed so dark and anguished and he grew distant, afraid of tomorrow,
His outbursts seemed more frequent, his language aggressive and bold

And I stayed awake at night and prayed, my soul
bruised and full of sorrow.

Oh when will my bonny boy return like a
fragrance from a flower
Pleasant, surprising and refreshing in the
majestic morning light,
His laughter and humor redemptive full of
innocence and power
My precious gift from God, my miracle and my
delight.

The Test of a Mother!

Privilege or duty, it comes at a higher cost
To instil beliefs that are right and good and just,
To love unconditionally if they are successful or waywardly lost
Privilege or duty-it's a deep lesson in trust.

Learning to question one's own moral void
To examine grey shadows and behaviour dark,
Searching for negative and repetitive patterns to avoid
Motherhood a lifelong journey on which you embark.

Teaching them to walk, talk, reason and rise
Nudging or pushing with kindness or subtle force,
The outcome unknown, failure, success or surprise
Trusting the process daily to avoid a lifetime of remorse.

This privilege or duty I accept with gladness and grace
May I teach them what is good, noble and pure,

Let me hold them tightly and learn to give them space
Privilege or duty- I accept and fully embrace.

Things that bring me Joy

The things that bring me the greatest joy in the world
Are fields full of peonies, wildflowers, fragrant and dew-pearled,
Dancing bees, swallows, larks and busy little hummingbirds
Little creatures feathered and winged that frolic undeterred.

The peace from watching the ocean as the waves keep pace
Frolicking white horses, the beach is my happy place,
Listening as the gurgling stream meanders away
My sorrow wiped and diluted by the effervescing spray.

The noise in my head calmed as I stand deep in the wood
The scent of pine heavy, my breathing deep as I feel more understood,
A ladybug deep red lands on a flower so pure and white
A contrasting vision so small but brings me sheer delight.

Yes, I find pleasure in a deep conversation with a true friend
But with the times and pace it's an uncommon trend,
I enjoy a high tea, a German apple cheesecake and I love to dine
The dawn and dusk farewelled with an exceptional blood red wine.

There is much to enjoy and more to revere
Both in good times and when harboring a tear,
Get away from my comfort zone and out of my head
To relish all that nature has birthed and be grateful instead.

I Have Been Here Before

Many a time I have been here before
Questioning and wondering and asking why,
What lies ahead and beyond this door?
Is this deep yearning my truth or a lie?

Many a time I have looked at my path
So many times, that it is hard to tell,
Each time I feel anguish and am filled with
wrath
Is it my fear or disappointment that I smell?

Around the mountain again and some more
Seeking and searching and hoping this is right,
From finance to teaching, from coaching to law
And with every acceptance my future seemed
bright.

Now I am melancholic, weary and tired
My hope for vocation waxing and waning, a
dream,
My spirit broken, bruised and so uninspired
My hopeful aspiration for contentment a vision
it would seem.

Oh, show me my destiny, my purpose my cause

Fill me with wisdom to discern my true way,
Let me find the road quietly without ado and applause
Guide me on this journey with certainty- this is for what I pray.

An Autumn Gift

It was late in my life that God gifted me my second child
With chubby cheeks and a gurgling smile,
Nothing like the first, less compliant a little wild
With an interesting mind and a unique style.

His humor is dry, quick and his laugh loud
His heart big and his feelings reflecting in his big blue eyes,
He sits alone when his spirit aggrieved, his eyes wet and head bowed
Such insight for his age, his words passionate and wise.

To think I questioned whether he was meant to be
Worried for his health and for mine at my age,
He has brought so much joy and merriment to me
And added years to my being if laughter is my gauge.

When they meet him, people say he will go far
Oil Barron, Entrepreneur or Businessman they say,

He is my larrikin, my lark, my little rising star
And he will always be my baby, no matter what one day.

I am grateful for this unexpected gift each and every second
And am relieved that I accepted to embrace this forceful little being,
Even though he was gifted as old age truly beckoned
The unequivocal experience could not have been prophesied or foreseen.

Anxiety-My old Friend

My dark thoughts and tightening chest steal my words
Anxiety is my mistress, she assures me this is my truth,
I am educated, well read and I believe her however absurd,
She has groomed and courted me, persistent since my youth.
She fills me with dread and fear with her false speaking tongue
As I grow older, I desire to disown her and cut all ties,
And I see her manipulation and genetics passed on to my son,
He too is held captive by her deceitful charm and endless lies.
I long for us both to languish in peace, clear headed like a sabbatical of rest
To resist her temptation, her tight grasp and suffocating hold,
To learn to pause, breathe, slow in the moment, this is the test,
To rewire our thoughts and train our brain to break the genetic mould.

To understand that anxiety comes like a thief to
steal your joy
She takes hold, tightens her grip leaving you
paralyzed, this is her ploy.

The Last Season

Middle-age bade me welcome and invited me in,
Time to reflect on my journey, its pleasure and sin,
The best way to do so with wine, cheese and gin.

As my children grow up and leave the nest,
As looks subside with drooping bum and breast,
It's time to embrace, not slow down or rest.

I dream to travel and reflect and write,
A new beginning, no time for adventure trite,
Elevating carpe diem to a whole new height.

On my tombstone let it be boldly said,
She was lively and wild and fairly well read,
The old girl shall be remembered even though she is dead.

My Mom

My mom afflicted with lupus and pain
Her limbs feeble, her body in waste,
Her mind strong and perfectly sane
And sometimes she prays for death in haste.

With each year her body lean and pale
She searches for answers and questions why,
Her atrophying muscles, she is stooped and frail
A burden to bare till possibly her death.

Yet she has held the faith and her resolve is
strong
Her spirit could be filled with sorrow, hate and
fear,
She could choose to ponder all that is wrong
Yet she spends her time praying for all she holds
dear.

So I acknowledge a life lived in pain now and
after
The bravest songs birthed from the saddest tear,
Yet in spite of the sorrow, she still embraces
laughter
Faithful and committed as the end draws near.

The Lie

It tells you that you are average and your looks are not the best
It tells you that you are not worthy and it would be better to die,
It tells you that you don't fit in and you are not like the rest
Oh please don't believe it, it is all a perpetual lie.

It tells you that you are stupid and your brain a little dim
It tells you that you are ugly and simply way to tall,
It tells you that your success and career chance is slim
It tells you that you're average, but that's ok, less chance to fall.

It tells you that you are a stranger, a lonely passing guest
And not to expect or harbour any great ambition,
It tells you to fear and not expect or want the best
It tells you mediocrity is normal, the human condition.

Oh please don't believe it and live in perpetual decay
Court your identity and to yourself be kind,
It's a lifelong journey that you must simply not delay
Knowing and loving oneself is indeed a true find.

Colours of Hope

I prayed and asked for a sign and oh what did I behold
A perfect rainbow in the sky,
And this is how we communicate if truth be told
And will be our call sign till the day that I die.

I have asked for direction from love to health
On emotional high and in the depths of despair,
I have prayed for guidance in poverty and wealth
Behold a rainbow acknowledgement of care.

I see your colour, my sign of hope
My mind at peace with happenings below,
And in the dazzling hue I can cope
Your presence radiating from the glow.

One True Love

A simple lad, a tradesmen who loved to fish
Who fell in love young when he had a head full of hair?
To make her his wife, that was his wish
His feelings true and his heart laid bare.

The family was uncertain and so he set her free
And tried to move on in love and life,
But try as he may, he could not let her be
His love life lacked commitment and was full of strife.

Years came and went and he worked, fished and drank
His heart held a void, a large open space,
Obliging the family as their wishes pulled rank
He realised his love for her he could not replace.

So after some 20 years and late in his life
He followed his heart under the African sun,
On a beach in Mazeppa Bay, he made her his wife
Like Camilla to Charles, she was always the one.

Scars of Migration

I have grown older and life organic as it is has
not shown me the essence of its seasons
It has not given me the hope in spring, the
feeling of what is next or best,
This year it is as if the river has frozen solid,
emotions trapped, no rhyme or reason
My hope encapsulated in ice, hard and cold has
but me too the test.

I have questioned my reason, my beginning and
my end
I have pondered natural justice and found it
wanting on earth,
The fragility of security and retribution I can
comprehend
And my hypnotic meanderings, I have relived
back to my birth.

I have dug deep and investigated what brings me
peace and joy
It's the whisper of meaningful conversation and
the connection of soul,
It's not the dance of deceit and a devious and
cunning ploy

Yet that lack of connection and understanding
has taken its toll.

I have found my answer in grief, the loss of what
tangible and true
A community of family and friends that
supported, encouraged and was kind,
I am connecting, finding, exploring but am not
true blue
I am seeking commonality, acceptance an
intellectual meeting of the mind.

Ten years on and for the first time in years on
some fronts, I am feeling the ice crack
I am expanding my circle, connections without
cultural boundary and definity,
Restoration seeps silently, slowly, the ice is
melting and perhaps I am coming back
The year of many firsts, dew on the petals, rain
on the depleted, little less despair for the trinity.

Life is choice, happiness is choice, but grief is
not always, grief is silent
She comes like an unwelcomed visitor and sits
at the table,
She picks her moments and when she does, she
brings paralysis and violence
She brings sadness, self-doubt, loss of
confidence as her visible label.

So tonight, we sit at her table, we confront, and
we stand
We welcome grief, we face her, and we pay bid
her goodbye
You have paid your rent, ruined the paint and
now it is time to vacate this land
The ice is melting, the current is vibrating, the
river will run on high.

Grace

Oh, that I should deserve and feel your
redemptive grace
My soul is burdened, heavy and entering the
early stages of rigor
I feel I have missed my call, this body an empty
vessel longing for your embrace
My emotions conflicting, suffocating and dark
rising and falling with every trigger
You ask for not much more than a commitment
to believe and commit to the race
A transaction so simple and pure yet so very
trying in the genre and sentiment of today
In a climate that calls for acceptance, tolerance
and agility in belief at an ever-changing pace
Belief in your modest and integral values have
become minimalized, mocked, viewed with
dismay
In our seeking to find acceptance and define a
blueprint that gives consent to who we have
become
We lose ourselves gradually and we seek to
delegate our emotional insecurity and apportion
blame
Our fragile spirits becoming bitter and tired as
we forge to change rhetoric and then some

Yet in spite of our heroic stance, we lose
connection, empathy and are somehow bondage
to shame
Oh, if we could only find our true self, an
identity full of purpose that requires no
justification
Where we live quietly, with bold compassion
without the need for recognition and affirmation.

Find your Tribe

We all need one, that very special lady that we can call friend
Sometimes we take her call and sometimes that identifying ring we choice to ignore,
She is the one that we call to share both news good and bad
She is your preference when you sit idle, or when you choose to explore.

You can call her at sunrise or send her that woeful text as you retreat to bed
When you tell her your world is collapsing and that your vocation has died,
You can share your anguish over disappointing children and a love unrequited
And she nods and soothes and grunts as if a soliloquy, sufficient as if she had replied.

I feel blessed for the many friends that have splashed my path with fragrance and dance
There is Jacqui, Jenny, Heather, Kristen, Desire, Louise, Michelle, Mandy, Sarah, Lesaya and Kim,
Just a few that have wrapped me in their arms and accepted that which in unequivocally me

These women, my pillars of strength, quirky,
humorous and different and by no account dim.

Oh, find your tribe in grandmothers, mothers
and maidens and linger in their presence
Don't throw the gift away over flippant word or
misunderstood intent,
Drink deeply from the fountain and accept them
as they are, there very essence
Your tribe, your angels, the gift of friendship- a
god sent.

www.ingramcontent.com/pod-product-compliance
Lightning Source LLC
Chambersburg PA
CBHW062203160726
48282CB00027B/976
9789357616966